DEAD TRUE CRIME

1

SACRIFICIAL
AXE

Voodoo Cult Slayings in the Deep South

C.J. MARCH

SLINGSHOT
BOOKS

Louisiana, 1909

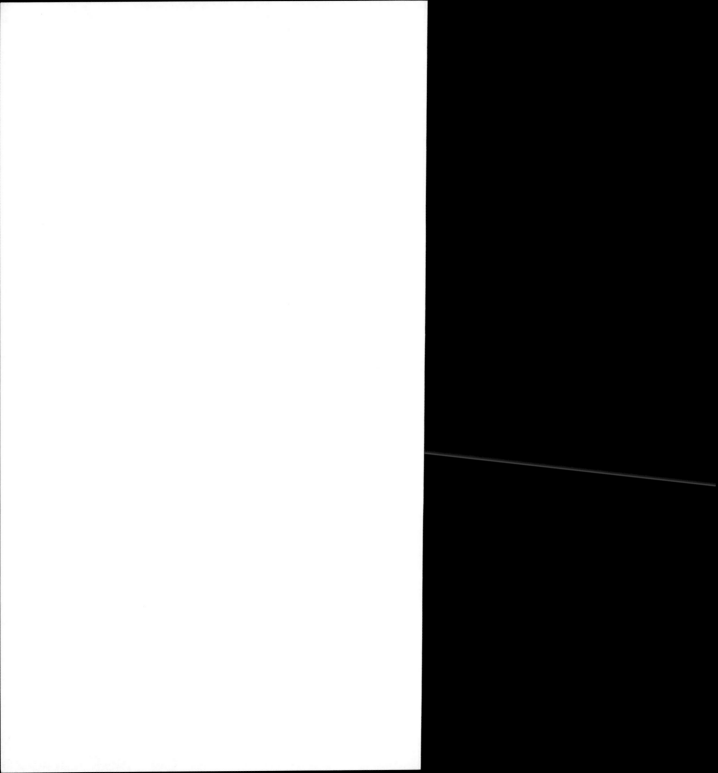

Edna Opelousas looked out the window of the dirt-floored hut. Thankfully, the ground under her feet was dry. The sky outside was calm, in stark contrast to the relentless nights when the Grand Isle hurricane chewed up southern Louisiana. It had been a long season of storms that tore siding off houses and soaked the ground beneath the clusters of shacks in the poor "negro quarters" of towns.

When the Grand Isle arrived, named for the town just south of New Orleans where the storm hit land, the hurricane ripped apart five thousand homes with winds of over eighty miles an hour and walls of rain spinning counter-clockwise around its center, and it didn't rest until it reached Missouri. It killed over 350 people and left a flooded landscape of wrecked homes, useful for little more than kindling. Predictably, the hardest hit by the disaster were poor and black.

Edna was both. That her ten-by-twelve-foot house in the township of Rayne hadn't been destroyed in the hurricane was a mercy, if not a miracle. It stood in the yard of her father's house, where he and her sister lived. The shacks of her neighbors started not twenty feet from her own walls, and the church was fifty feet away. There was little privacy. When Edna turned from the window to usher her kids into bed, she knew that her neighbors could hear every noise they made.

Aged four to nine years old, they all shared the one bed the family had in the cramped space of the room.

The sun had set on the little neighborhood in Rayne and night was bearing down on the entire Acadia Parish. Edna blew out the candle and joined her kids in bed, the only light coming from the half-moon cut out of the black November sky.

A few hours later, her sister was startled out of sleep by the sound of someone opening the door of Edna's shack. Looking out the window, her sister saw, in the faint glow of the moon, a figure going in through the door. She went to wake their father. Outside, the familiar Louisiana lullaby: the whir and creak of insects; the throaty calls of frogs. Then she heard Edna's oldest daughter scream.

Still in their nightclothes, Edna's sister and father ran into the yard in time to see a man leave Edna's shack. With his hat in his hand, he ran south. Instead of running after him, they went to check on Edna and the kids. Neighbors, hearing the screams, came out of their shacks to see what had happened, to help if they could.

They could see it all from the door of the one-room shack. Edna was on the floor, covered in blood. Her head had been split open with an ax. The packed dirt underneath her was darkening as she bled out. The three children, their heads hacked in the same way, blood and brains smeared all over the small room. Near the door was the ax, which police would determine had been stolen from the yard of a neighbor a couple of blocks away. It was sticky with the warm blood of the family.

Edna was dead, but the children were still breathing, barely alive. Edna's family and neighbors were frantic. They rushed the children to a doctor, but the way was rough and slow, the damage inflicted by the killer extensive. Every single child died within a day.

At the scene of the "fiendish crime," Sheriff Louis Fontenot and Coroner Hines C. Webb found only "slight clues," and the sheriff at first declared the motive a mystery. After questioning family and neighbors, though, he found out that a woman had allegedly threatened Edna with an ax and had just recently been in custody for striking her. He arrested Estelle Washington and her parents, George and America, but quickly released them. The distance between an argument and the slaughter of a whole family with an ax was vast, and there was no evidence that Estelle had or would do such a thing. Her threat had been an idle one.

When Fontenot told the newspapers that the details were "meager," it would be fair to question the resources the authorities devoted to the case. The person seen running from Edna's shack was black and Edna and her children were black. Many of the newspapers covering the murders didn't even bother to record the victims' names. This was 1909 Louisiana and there may have been scant will to solve a bizarre murder in the poorest neighborhood of Rayne. Fontenot likely believed it to be a gruesome, but isolated incident. But the Opelousas family killing was the beginning of a series of ax murders that would terrify African American communities in Louisiana and Texas for the next two years.

Not ten miles from Rayne and the site of the first murder lay Crowley, Louisiana. Whereas Rayne was known for its frogs exported by rail to restaurants in New Orleans, Crowley was famous for rice. By 1911, the rice fields of Crowley were producing more than half a million bags each year and the rice mills processed fifteen thousand barrels a day. The claypan prairie soil of the area was perfect for growing the grain, and there were plenty of workers to harvest, hull, and polish. The job was tedious and grueling for the black workers, even with the hulling machines. The challenge for white Southerners in the post–Reconstruction South was that they now had to pay for labor. But not that much.

Walter Byers was one of those laborers in "Rice City." Every day, for his meager wages, Byers came home grimy and exhausted from the United States Mill near the railroad to his wife, Silvina, and their six-year-old son. The rice mill was one of the largest employers in Crowley. If you didn't work at the rice mill, you likely worked for the railroad or on a farm outside of town. The western side of Crowley, the black side, where Byers and his family lived, was referred to as "Coontown," as were most black quarters across the South. Popularized by the song "Zip Coon" that was played at minstrel shows in the 1830s, the word is believed to have originated from the Portuguese word *barracão* or the Spanish word *barracón* (anglicized to barracoon), which referred to a large building constructed to hold merchandise, where slaves were kept for sale. Now these neighborhoods held the blacks, keeping them separate from the whites.

Slavery had been abolished by the Thirteenth Amendment in 1865, less than forty-five years earlier. By 1870, 15 percent of all elected officials in the South were black. In 1897, 130,344 black men were registered to vote in the state of Louisiana (women would have to wait another twenty-three years to legally cast a ballot). It seemed as though the aspirations of these new citizens, and of the abolitionists and the civil rights minded, would be achieved. But the optimism of those years directly following the Civil War would wither with the passage of racist Jim Crow laws, or "black codes," radically restricting the rights of blacks.

The very name "Jim Crow" had a racist origin. Before the Civil War, a white actor named Thomas Dartmouth "Daddy" Rice created a character named Jim Crow for his minstrel show after witnessing an elderly black slave singing the song "Jump Jim Crow" in Louisville, Kentucky. Donning blackface, Rice portrayed a distorted, bumbling stereotype of a black slave. It was a huge hit with white audiences and set the mold for countless minstrel acts to follow. Whites began to use the epithet "Jim Crow" to refer to blacks, and later, the term gave more than a clue to the antiblack character of the laws state legislatures were passing.

By 1900, even though 47 percent of Louisiana was black, the number registered to vote dropped to 5,320—over 125,000 fewer than three years before. By 1910, that number was 730, less than the population of the small town of Rayne, Louisiana. The effects of the Jim Crow laws were long lasting and pernicious. In 1940, there were still only 847 African Americans in Louisiana registered to vote.

Segregating blacks from the white public sphere, Jim

Crow laws encoded the caste system slavery began, but with a rhetorical flourish: "separate but equal" made it sound as though blacks would enjoy the same privileges as whites, just not in the same spaces. The truth was far bleaker. Invariably, the facilities for African Americans were underfunded and inferior. The black codes kept the community disenfranchised and impoverished. Jim Crow was the law of the land in towns like Rayne and Crowley. Edna Opelousas, Walter Byers, and the other blacks of Louisiana lived under the yoke of that law.

The Byers lived in a simple house, the wooden door hanging loosely on its hinges. They made do. It was easier with just one child in such a small space. Around 6:30 p.m., one of the Byers' neighbors saw Silvina through the window and waved. Night was coming on and everyone was finishing chores and beginning the evening routine. Beyond the roof lines, the sun was sinking, burning orange over the rice fields and the train tracks.

Walter and Silvina tucked their six-year-old son into bed after dinner. Shortly after, under a dusky sky, the Byers blew out the candles and joined their son in sleep.

The little girl skipped through the dirt as she ran her errands. Paying a visit to the Byers family was next. Walter Byers hadn't shown up at work and no one had seen the family for days. Approaching the house, the child almost turned around, suddenly sick to her stomach. The odor coming from the Byers' place was rancid, the smell of something rotting. The door was locked. Something was wrong. The girl ran for help.

The Byers family were lying in one bed, their skulls split open with an ax. Walter and Silvina were lying next to each other; their little boy stretched out at their feet. The bed was awash in blood and bloody footprints covered the floor. At the top of the bed lay the ax used to kill them, the metal head caked with blood, the wooden handle stained with it. The bowl on the washstand was half filled with bloody water: the murderer had washed their hands before leaving the Byers' house. The family had been dead nearly three days.

When Coroner Webb (the coroner in the Opelousas investigation), Chief Marshal Lyons, and two of his deputies, Officers Ballew and Higginbotham, arrived, they were overpowered by the stench. Stepping away from the house, Lyons demanded powerful disinfectants to neutralize the odor, compromising the crime scene and any evidence they might find.

The door was locked from the inside. The killer had come in through the window and bludgeoned a sleeping Walter in his bed. Silvina had been butchered on the floor during an attempt to save her son and get away—the footprints were hers. Then she was laid on the bed next to her husband, their child at their feet, before the killer rinsed their hands in the water that had been left in the washbowl the night before.

These details were of little help to Lyons. His questioning led first to Ed Jackson, a black man who allegedly had been "mixed up" with the family for some time. Lyons arrested him, hoping that he could close the case and be done with the "coontown axe murder." But Jackson was soon released for lack of evidence, or any real indication that he would commit an act so violent. Rumors that Walter had made enemies at the Baptist church the family attended went nowhere. He was secretary of the church; he was considered reputable and generally peaceable.

Though he'd also had a fight with a man at the rice mill, which led to the man getting fired, the two men had shaken hands and made up, so that lead was a dead end as well. Lyons and his investigators were looking for motives in the family's relationships with their neighbors and coworkers. They were looking in the wrong place. Only weeks later, another family would be slaughtered. This time a detail of the crime scene would point to a dark religious or cult connection.

Voodoo haunted the American South. Supposed eyewitness accounts of voodoo rituals appeared regularly in nineteenth-century newspapers. The articles confirmed what many whites believed to be true about blacks, emphasizing savagery, hypersexuality, and imperiled white womanhood. They underlined the dangers of allowing blacks too much power. The stories featured fetish and demon worship, animal sacrifice, cannibalism, and orgies.

Many blacks feared and believed in its power, not least to counter the ongoing oppression by whites. Whites believed in it, too. Particularly in its potential to empower blacks. Driven by fear and control—fear of the new black citizenry and a demand for control that would echo the caste system of slavery—whites in power would use specious tales of voodoo to scare up support for repressive Jim Crow laws. Invoking voodoo—its fearsome power and depravities—would prove a potent tool in the fight to re-enslave blacks in effect if not in name.

Louisiana had its own flavor of voodoo, often called New Orleans Voodoo, with Creole French as its liturgical language. Emphasizing amulets, objects of power known as "candjas" or "hoodoos," and voodoo queens, New Orleans Voodoo took hold of the area and still lives on in the cultural imagination. The gris-gris, a small cloth bag that functioned as a talisman, was believed to protect the wearer from harm or bring good luck. Voodoo provided a way for practitioners to protect themselves, take revenge, exercise power in the world controlled by whites—a world that was as dangerous as the magic of voodoo seemed to be. Voodoo in the nineteenth century was also dominated by free women of color.

White supremacists were terrified of it and considered voodoo both a literal and symbolic threat of "Negro domination." In 1886, the city government deemed the number of "Voodoo professionals" in New Orleans to be so worrisome that the Board of Health tried to intervene. And during the late 1900s, there was fear of the "measureless influence" voodoo priests would have on "executive and legislative authorities and ignorant voters." Voodoo in the white imagination was a real and rising menace. The next crime scene in the string of ax murders would have terrified anybody—white or black, believer or non-believer.

A lexander Andrus spent his days at the end of a shovel pushing coal to fuel the steam locomotives that came through Lafayette, a town twenty-five miles to the east of Crowley. The job at the Southern Pacific roundhouse was hot and dirty, and Andrus returned home at night coated in coal dust. He lived with his wife, Mimi, and their two children, Joachim, three, and Agnes, not yet a year old, in the Doucet-Trahan area of Lafayette near the Lafayette sugar refinery. The house was just beyond the Southern Pacific Railroad track, a short walk to work for Alexander.

Newspaper photograph of the Andrus home.

At midnight one Saturday in February, while the Andrus family was sleeping, someone came in through the kitchen door carrying an ax. Alexander and Mimi were dispatched quickly, hacked to death before they even woke up. Joachim was brained with the weapon. Then the killer crushed baby Agnes' head while she lay in her cradle. In the other murders, the killer immediately fled the scene. But tonight, the killer pulled Alexander and Mimi onto the floor, bent their knees and leaned them up against the bed, adjusting their nightclothes and arms.

When Mimi's brother, Lezime Felix, stopped by the Andrus home at 7 a.m. the next morning, he found his sister and brother-in-law arranged as if praying. Mimi's arm was draped over Alexander's shoulder and the two of them were kneeling against their bed. Their bodies were still warm.

Sheriff Louis LaCoste was called to the scene and, as in the case of the previous murders, the police found no meaningful clues. LaCoste was a striking man, his prominent mustache like dark, tapered wings stretching across his face.

He had been sheriff for six years and knew the parish well. Seeing the killing as madness, he thought of an "escaped lunatic" from Pineville named Garcon Godfry. The man was found and arrested but was in another town at the time and had a solid alibi. He was sent back to the asylum.

Photograph of Sheriff Louis LaCoste.

The police of Louisiana were no closer to solving the murders. The arrangement of the family in a gesture of prayer escalated the panic already building in the black neighborhoods. A motive of jealousy or revenge would contain the murders to the circle of the killer, but slaughter prompted by religiosity or cult beliefs had no bounds. Nobody was safe. The speculation that these were voodoo crimes would only build momentum when a family of five was killed in San Antonio, Texas.

Hyped up as the specter of voodoo may have been, in the case of these murders, there was reason to talk about voodoo, reason to worry about the hoodoo, and reason to lock the door.

After slaughtering the Cassaway family in San Antonio, the killer covered their faces with cloth, as though performing some funeral rite. A blanket had been hung over the north window of the house. The authorities quickly dismissed any robbery motive. Not a single drawer in the bureau or wardrobe had been opened and nothing had been taken. Louis Cassaway's pants were hanging off the foot of the bed, money in the pockets. His watch was still in his vest. All three children, the youngest five months old, were battered to death with the blunt side of the ax. The bodies had been arranged in a manner one newspaper described as "almost lovingly." The family was lined up in order of biggest to smallest and then covered up with blankets. The killing had spread to eastern Texas.

Sheriff LaCoste spoke with the authorities in San Antonio, comparing notes on the murders in both states. They all believed that the killings were committed by the same person, someone using the Southern Pacific Railroad to get around.

Despite the fact that a killer couldn't travel with an ax on the train, it was a convenient tool for wholesale slaughter. Every poor family would have kept an ax by the woodpile; they survived by wood fires, keeping warm in the cold, damp winters, cooking over them all year long. Newspapers reported that people slept with the family ax under the bed.

No need to bring a murder weapon when your victims or their neighbors kept one handy for you.

Alexander Andrus had worked in the Southern Pacific coal chutes before his death. Questioning coworkers of Andrus at the roundhouse, LaCoste learned of Raymond Barnabet. According to rumors, there was "bad blood between them," and the men had fought. Still, it would be six months before LaCoste brought Barnabet in for questioning.

Raymond Barnabet lived with two of his grown children, Clementine and Zepherin, on a farm six miles south of Rayne, not far from where Edna Opelousas and her children had been killed. Raymond made the trip into Lafayette for work at the Southern Pacific. His other children, Noah, Pauline, Ferran, and Tatite, had moved off the farm but lived close by. LaCoste would arrest the entire family before the investigation was complete.

Estranged from his wife, Raymond had a poor reputation. He was carrying on a relationship with a woman named Diana, who told a friend that she thought he was the ax murderer based on things he said when he was drunk. Diana would later defend Raymond and tell the police that her friend had misunderstood.

LaCoste hauled Raymond to the brick jail in Lafayette and kept him separate from the other witnesses in the case. From the beginning, Raymond protested his innocence. There was no evidence that he had killed the Andrus family, let alone any of the other families slaughtered in Louisiana and Texas. At first, his arrest appeared to be as much of a dead end as that of the other arrests the police had made in the previous ax murder cases. Then LaCoste questioned Raymond's children.

Nineteen-year-old Clementine was of "striking stature." One reporter compared her to the World Heavyweight Champion wrestler Frank Gotch. She told the sheriff that their father hadn't come home after work the night of the Andrus murders. Her brother Zepherin corroborated her story. They waited for Raymond, they said, for hours. Then, sometime after 2 a.m., he stormed into the Barnabet house "in a rage," his clothes, hands, and face covered in blood. Rousing them from their beds, he forced them to help him clean up and launder his clothes to hide the evidence. Clementine and Zepherin both said that Raymond told them that he would kill them if they told a soul. LaCoste had what he needed to go to the district attorney, and Raymond Barnabet was charged with murder.

Just weeks after his arrest, Raymond was taken from the jail on a boneshaking ride in a wagon over the beaten dirt roads of the town. He arrived at the Lafayette Parish Courthouse drunk. Indicted for the murders of the entire Andrus family, Raymond was tried only for the killing of the year-old child. The prosecution, District Attorney John J. Robira, may have been betting that the most horrific of the crimes, the grisly murder of a baby, would surely bring a conviction. After arresting Raymond, LaCoste and his deputies had returned to the Barnabet farm but found only some blood on a dress of Clementine's that she said was from cleaning her father's clothes. All the prosecution had was the testimony of Clementine and her brother Zepherin.

On the stand, Clementine's and Zepherin's testimonies were inconsistent and muddled. Court officials began to doubt the credibility of the story. Sitting with his defense attorney, George P. Lessley, an unkempt Raymond Barnabet was wobbly and glassy-eyed as he listened to the accusations of his children. Lessley told the judge that Raymond couldn't testify in his own defense because he was drunk. Between this and the erratic stories of his kids, the trial was such a shambles that some expected a mistrial. The jury, though, believed Clementine and Zepherin and found their father guilty of murdering an infant.

In his frustration at the defendant's state, Judge William Campbell couldn't help "lashing out at the bailiff, the jailor and the sheriff." But Raymond's drinking that day would save his life. Campbell had intended to sentence him to death for the murder, but the confusion of the proceedings and Raymond's drunken state gave him pause. Instead of sending him to the gallows, he granted a new trial and sent him back to jail.

Raymond Barnabet was sitting behind bars awaiting a new trial when the Randall family was axed to death in Lafayette, not far from the Andrus family house.

It was raining in Lafayette that night, a steady downpour playing music on the roof of Norbert and Azema Randall's house and soaking the ground. Raised up on blocks, the house's wood floor kept all but the flooding of a hurricane from reaching their feet, and the Randalls could sleep easy knowing that the storm outside wouldn't threaten them in their beds.

Everybody liked the Randalls. They were considered one of the "best families" in the black neighborhood of Mills. Instead of a single-room shack, they lived in a three-room house with a shallow porch on the front and a narrow set of steps that led up from the ground. But there were rumors: they'd attended a Sacrifice Church service near their home, a service in which voodoo may have played a part.

Newspaper photograph of the Randall home.

Norbert and Azema were still mourning the deaths of the Andrus family. Mimi Andrus was Azema's sister. The families lived close, and it had been a matter of days since their three-year-old nephew and baby niece had been buried. Norbert and Azema had four kids of their own. Their oldest daughter was spending the night at the house of an uncle and aunt, and their nephew, Albert, who was six, had come over for a sleep-over. The kids played before bed. Rene was the same age as Albert. Little Norbert was a year younger and Agnes was only two. Norbert and Azema tucked the kids under the blanket, settling their energy and urging them to go to sleep. Shortly after, they went to bed themselves in the other room. The killer came in through the back door of the shack, bringing an ax, dripping water on the floor from the storm. The modus operandi of the Randall murders was similar to the killings that preceded it, with one difference. Before the family was butchered with the ax, the killer shot Norbert in the face with a pistol. Maybe it was the sound of the gunshot that startled one of the kids awake. In the attempt to escape, the child left bloody footprints along the side of a bed. All the children were murdered, "their brains knocked out with an ax." No one escaped.

When the Randall's nine-year-old daughter came home in the morning under the continuing downpour, she found the door to the house open.

Inside, the bodies of her family lay "weltering in their blood." Their heads were "terribly crushed and blood and brains spattered over the room and bedding." Norbert, Azema, and one of the kids were on one bed. The three other children were piled together at the foot of another. Their faces and heads were horribly mutilated. Blood saturated the mattresses and bedding; blood covered the floor. The windows were flecked with it. Once again left behind, the ax leaned against the wall near the foot of the bed. This time the metal blade and wooden handle had been carefully washed off.

The sole surviving member of the family, Norbert and Azema's daughter ran to the neighbors, who called the police. A frustrated LaCoste arrived to examine the crime scene. Rain was still coming down outside, wiping away any trace of the escaping killer.

The next day, a woman joined the crowd gathering outside the Randall home. She laughed out loud at all the shocked and frightened people whispering and pulling their kids closer. Sheriff LaCoste heard the laughter and looked around to see who found the scene of such horror funny. He knew that woman. She'd just testified against her father.

Clementine Barnabet.

Sheriff LaCoste remembered the dress. When he'd found blood on Clementine Barnabet's dress the day he arrested Raymond Barnabet, she and Zepherin claimed that the blood came from the attempt to launder their father's clothes after he murdered the Andrus family. It had seemed plausible at the time, but now that another family had been slaughtered while Raymond Barnabet stewed behind bars, LaCoste reconsidered everything he'd been told by the Barnabet children.

LaCoste arrested Clementine and searched the farm again. He discovered that the latch string on the front gate of the house was soaked with blood. The police also found bloody clothing locked in Clementine's bedroom closet: a blue and white dress splattered with blood and pieces of tissue that looked like brains. She admitted they belonged to her. Confronted with the clothing, though, she laughed at the police and said that she had nothing to do with the deaths of the Randalls. Her seeming confidence and indifferent demeanor would be remarked on repeatedly and frustrate the police.

The community, though hopeful at the introduction of a new suspect, likely regarded the arrest skeptically. How could a woman, barely an adult, be capable of the nightmarish slaughter of men, women, and children? Of bashing in the skulls of babies sleeping in their cradles. How could this nine-teen-year-old possibly be the serial killer terrorizing the area?

Newspapers had begun to speculate about a cult, a group of people carrying out these murders. And police doubted that one person, particularly a woman of nineteen, could have successfully carried out multiple homicides of whole families across two states. Everyone doubted that she'd committed the crimes alone, even if her footsteps were "stealthy and catlike" and families who employed her said that she would often steal into a room unnoticed, surprising them. Sheriff LaCoste believed he had the right person. Or at least one of them.

On top of questions about the number of perpetrators, debate surrounded the victims. What, if anything, connected them? At one point the authorities thought that all the victims had once lived in Carencro, Louisiana, but that theory didn't stand up. It was obviously significant that all the victims were families, and so many of them children. If a cult had committed these crimes, it might explain the choice of victims.

Stories circulated that voodoo practitioners routinely sacrificed innocents in rituals worshipping the snake god, even drinking the child victim's blood to gain power. So-called eyewitness accounts of such practices were suspect. In the hands of the white press, voodoo was a race issue, whipping up fear of blacks post–Reconstruction, before Jim Crow once again codified their subjugation. The actual voodoo practices that existed in the southern United States probably would have been kept secret—no white witness would have been invited in to carry the story back to their newspaper.

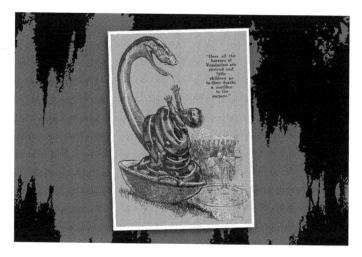

Newspaper illustration of voodoo rituals.

In the black community, the specter of dark magic, the twisting of religious practices from their families' diverse homelands into bloody and violent ritual, haunted them. Given the miasma of fear and sensationalism swirling around the serial ax murders, common superstition and the use of charms merged with dark fantasy. But the mutilated bodies of twenty-two people were no fantasy, just a horrifying mystery.

Clementine impassively maintained her innocence, appearing unbothered by the accusations. LaCoste arrested other members of her family, including her half sister, Pauline, who lived in Rayne. Pauline's movements were considered suspicious; LaCoste believed she was an accessory. Pauline claimed to know very little of her sister and, eventually, the sheriff had to release her.

LaCoste and his deputies felt increasing pressure to solve the case. Blacks were moving out of the neighborhoods in the area, afraid for their lives and the lives of their families. The exodus put a strain on rice production; newspapers as far away as New York reported on the potential economic impact.

Based on the ritualistic character of the slayings, especially the Andrus family crime scene, police began investigating religious groups in the area. In Louisiana, it was illegal for more than three African Americans to congregate without the express consent of the authorities.

One sect drew their attention and the speculation of newspapers. The Christ Sanctified Holy Church was a relatively new organization, with congregations in several towns along the Southern Pacific Railroad, including Lake Charles, Crowley, and Lafayette, all locations of ax murders. The church was called both the "Sanctified Church" and, forebodingly, the "Church of Sacrifice." That moniker alone likely drew the scrutiny of the police.

Sheriff LaCoste discovered that the group had held a religious meeting near the Randall house on the night the family was murdered, one that the Randalls were rumored to have attended. Convinced that they were involved in the murders, but unable to prove a connection, he kept several members of the church under surveillance.

Reverend King Harrison had been proselytizing across southern Louisiana, expanding the footprint of the order. LaCoste arrested him, but the preacher denied that any of the church's doctrine encouraged crime or murder. Rejecting the accusation that the church had voodoo elements, he maintained that he preached the New Testament.

But police pursued the connection because of the perceived "religious fanaticism" of the crimes, and contended that, even if the organization did not openly encourage criminal practices, "the negroes are so intensely moved and impressed by the teaching of the testament sacrificial ideas and ceremonies that they are incited to commit atrocious crimes." One newspaper claimed that "the creed of the sect is a curious mixture of African voodoo rites, superstitions of American Indians and of ignorant French, English, and Spanish settlers, and strangest of all, a so-called religion based upon Holy Writ, deriving its power from the distorted and garbled interpretation of the Bible common to all the illiterate negroes of the South."

The Church of Sacrifice was compared to the "Council of God" sect of New Orleans. The Council of God was associated with the stabbing of a white storekeeper's wife, the killing of a police officer, and the shooting death of the group's leader. Reverend Harrison acknowledged a similarity between the sects.

Another preacher was arrested and, according to police, admitted to a sanctification doctrine—that when people "become sanctified they can no longer sin against God, no matter what crimes and murder they might commit." The officers demanded that he provide the names of his converts.

Police conducted what were called "third degree" interrogations, with no details on what that entailed. Writing at the turn of the century, former police chief Richard Sylvester defined the first degree as the arrest, the second as the transport to incarceration, the third, the interrogation. Whatever the origins of the term, historically the third degree has almost certainly been a euphemism for police brutality. In 1912, suspects in the ax-man murders likely did not meet with gentle handling, and all that could be done to secure a confession had no doubt been done.

Rough treatment notwithstanding, Clementine took a "sphinxlike attitude" and continued to deny any involvement. Newspapers reported, "though confident that she's guilty, the police begin to question whether they will be able to get her to confess." Things took an even bleaker turn when, with Clementine secure in her cell and Raymond in his, the "ax-man" struck again.

7

It was a wintry day in Promised Land. Harriet Crane knocked on the door of the two-room shack her daughter Marie Warner lived in with her three children in the aspirationally named neighborhood of Crowley. Marie had her hands full, a single mother separated from the children's father, who lived all the way in Beaumont, Texas.

Harriet must have been eager to get inside her daughter's house on such a cold day. No one answered her knocks. The door was locked. Harriet went next door where the neighbor, Dorsey Berdsong, told her she hadn't seen the family and didn't know where they'd gone. Maybe Harriet knew right then something was wrong. Maybe Marie had been expecting her, so why wouldn't she be home? Where would they all have gone in such weather? Harriet persuaded Ben Robinson, another Promised Land neighbor, to find a way into the house and check on the family.

Robinson found Marie Warner and her kids face down on the bed. They'd been axed to death in their sleep.

That January of 1912, Sheriff LaCoste and his colleagues in parishes terrorized by ax murders were grasping at straws. Police brought a pack of bloodhounds to the Warner crime scene, intending to unleash them on the trail of the killer. The ground around the house was "so trampled up," though, that the police weren't sure any scent the dogs picked up would be the right one. Nonetheless, there were two more swift arrests. Another preacher, Reverend Joseph Wilkins, and Eliza Richards, a friend of Marie Warner's, were taken into custody. They were confined in separate jails in neighboring parishes to keep them apart. But it was clear that the police had no solid leads and were just trying to demonstrate activity on the case.

Fear within the black neighborhoods was palpable. The police had promised them twice that the culprits of the wholesale slaughters had been captured, yet the killings continued. A mass meeting was called, and the black community adopted resolutions "expressive of the desire and intentions of the race to do all in its power to uncover the perpetrators of these horrible butcheries."

After a similar meeting at the Morning Star Baptist Church, an attendee said that "No violator of the law, nor 'Voo Doo' unable to tell the mystery of the ax, could have felt safe after these speeches." ("Voo Doo" here refers both to the practice and the practitioner.) Empowering as the speeches may have been, there was little the community could actually do to protect themselves. People armed themselves to the extent they were able. They kept vigil every night, and there were frequent reports of break-in attempts, most of which were the false alarms of fearful people. As an alarm system, some people "ran fishing lines from their toes to their doorknobs." Many left their homes to sleep at their neighbors' houses; black domestics took to sleeping in their white employers' kitchens. And others left the rice belt entirely, putting as much distance between themselves and the ax murderer as possible.

White employers bemoaned the effect of the murders on their employees. Their domestics—many of them former slaves who stayed on with their "masters" even when legally emancipated—were packing their few belongings and leaving the area. White planters worried about a labor shortage when the rice was ready to harvest. And as black men armed themselves, whites feared what would happen once the murders had passed into memory. An armed community of black folk was an existential threat to the white status quo.

Many whites were convinced the ax murders were separate, unrelated incidents. Some even used the spreading terror to play cruel jokes on black people. And in a meeting led by white authorities, they tried to convince the black community the ax man was a figment of their collective imagination. Still, out of that meeting came a petition to the governor of Louisiana for funds to put up a reward for the capture of the murderer. Governor Jared Young Sanders was up for re-election. With so few blacks registered or able to vote, the reward of $500 he authorized was likely a gesture for white employers. Still, the black community adopted a resolution to formally thank the governor and the white community for their help.

Then, one night, in the town of Lake Charles, the killer raised the stakes.

⊂━⊂━⊃

Felix Broussard was sound asleep next to his wife, Margaret, on a corn husk mattress. Their children, Albert, aged six, and Louis, aged three, were sleeping in a nearby room. The temperature would dip down to nineteen degrees before the night was over. The cabin was big by the standards of the neighborhood: two rooms and a separate kitchen. It stood a few hundred yards from the Lake Charles Rice Mill and within fifty feet of the Kansas City Southern Railroad switch line. The train tracks curved right through their backyard. Lake Charles was still rebuilding after a devastating fire downtown just a couple of years before, but rice and the railroad continued to be the twin engines of the town's growth. The Broussards were probably used to sleeping through the noise of trains and industry in that busy area. They might not have woken up at the sound of an intruder.

With all the new construction going on, Felix was busy in his job as foreman at a sawmill. He was doing well by his family. He had a $20 life insurance policy for each of his children. An "industrious" man, Felix was, like so many of the victims, "without enemies."

That night, their next-door neighbor, Victoria Northern, was up cooking until one thirty in the morning. She'd seen the Broussards light a lamp around dark but didn't see them after that. When she got up in the morning, she noticed that the Broussards' back door was open and "thought that a little strange." She asked her husband to go knock on the door and call them. No one answered; he told Victoria he was going to go in the house. "No," she told him. "Get an officer."

Just then, another neighbor, Mrs. Thibodeaux, stopped by to borrow milk and told Victoria of her "uneasiness for the Broussard family." Her husband, J.C. Thibodeaux, finally looked in the wide-open back door. He saw "the leg of a child protruding" from under clothing in one of the bedrooms.

The killer had come in through the kitchen window and brought an ax. Felix's own ax was found in the kitchen unused and clean. The skulls of Felix and Margaret and their two children were crushed in; their heads battered almost to a pulp. Brains were smeared over the bedclothes, the floor, and the walls. The ax was found underneath the bed, "besmeared" with blood.

Before the murderer killed the children, they put a bucket below their heads to catch the dripping blood. The fingers of each hand of the victims had been stretched apart, "those of the children wedged open with paper and fastened with pins."

And this time, there was a message. On the door, the killer wrote: "When he maketh the inquisition for blood, he forgetteth not the cry of the humble." An incomplete passage from the Bible: Psalm 9:12. To the side of the inscription was scrawled "Human 5."

Newspaper drawing of Broussard victim's hand.

That a cult was behind the spate of slaughters now seemed clear. Theories abounded. People speculated that the murderers wanted to kill in sets of five, adhering to the "mysticism of the figure five which has always been held by primitive people." The killings of families of four or six were explained away: the killers had believed there were five people in the family, or some event or unexpected incident had changed the number of people in the house at the time of each murder.

Newspapers explained the mystery of how whole families could be murdered without much struggle and without alerting the neighbors in houses that were practically on top of each other by conjecturing that some of the victims had been willing participants in the ritual. And some even suggested that the cross, with its four points and center, represented the number five and that was why voodoo practitioners attended Christian churches. This contention supported continued investigation of the Christian sects in the area. The arrests continued.

Dr. A. E. Anderson was detained for "suspicious" travel in the area. Anderson was a member of the Church of Sacrifice. Another man, Ed Jiles, was arrested and put in a "sweat box." From his own long experience as a police chief, Richard Sylvester described the sweat box in lurid terms, as a cell with a monster stove adjoining, into which vegetable matter, old bones, pieces of rubber shoes and kindred trophies would be thrown, all to make a terrible heat, offensive as it was hot, to at last become so torturous and terrible as to cause the sickened and perspiring object of punishment to reveal the innermost secrets he possessed as the compensation for release from the "sweat box."

The sweat box had been used since the lawless time following the Civil War, as an attempt to curb the activities of the "marauder, the bank robber and the highwayman, thieves and criminals of every kind." More than likely, Ed Jiles had nothing to confess, but probably wouldn't be the last suspect in the investigation of the ax murders to end up in the box.

Meanwhile, the slaughter continued. Weeks after the Broussard murders, Hattie Dove and her three children headed to bed on a Sunday night. Ernest and Ethel were teenagers, just a couple of years separating them. Jessie was eighteen but had moved back home after separating from her husband. Her mother might have some sympathy with that decision, herself separated from Jessie's father. Struggling to make ends meet, Hattie had taken in a boarder who worked nights. The family lived in the north end of Beaumont, Texas, just a block west of the Magnolia Avenue Baptist Church. It was 9:30 p.m. and the family was settling in for the night.

Two blocks away, an ax had been left in a yard. That ax was found along with the bodies of the Dove family the next morning. Shortly before 7 a.m., a neighbor came by the Dove house and found Hattie and her children butchered. Near the ax was the cloth the murderer had used to wipe off bloody hands.

Black ministers, teachers, doctors, and businessmen met

to discuss what could be done. One meeting in Lake Charles, the site of the Broussard family murder, spoke directly about the failure of the white police:

> Whereas we appreciate the efforts of our own officers and of those cities, where the crimes have been committed, to protect their colored citizens against these blood-thirsty demons and bring the perpetrators to justice, we therefore feel that there ought to be some demonstration on our part to assist them.

> Whereas the ax-man has paralyzed the domestic, industrial, social, and religious life among the negroes here and in those sections where his viciousness has been displayed, we therefore solicit funds from every race lover, peace preserver and law abiding colored citizen of Lake Charles to assist in arresting this maniac.

The killings "stirred all Southwest Louisiana with mystery and fear of the return of the fiend who wields an axe with a viciousness no less horrible than it is unexpected and unwarranted." Thousands turned out to see the Dove family at their memorial. "Many of them moaned that the Lord had deserted them and some of them were heard to murmur that a curse had falled [sic] upon their race."

Eight seemingly random families had been viciously murdered, thirty-four people in all, twenty-one of them children between infancy and sixteen years old. The terror the white authorities had hoped would be fleeting took root in the area's black neighborhoods. A few nights after the Dove murders, a woman heard a noise at her front door and "shot through the panel without taking the trouble to enquire what she was shooting at."

The police, however, were about to get the answers they'd long been looking for. From Clementine Barnabet, who'd been sitting in her cell while Marie Warner and Hattie Dove and their children were hacked to death.

C lementine may have been in jail when the most recent murders took place, but Sheriff LaCoste still believed she was involved. Some floated the idea that the murders were a plot by the Human Five to clear Clementine. The sheriff also believed she was responsible for the Andrus family killing. Their murder might have been an attempt to frame Raymond Barnabet. But with the killers still on the loose, how could Clementine be convicted?

LaCoste enlisted the help of Professor A.L. Metz, a chemist and blood expert in New Orleans, to examine Clementine's bloody clothing. Metz confirmed that the blood and material found on Clementine's clothing were human blood and human brains, and the same as that from the Randall cabin. How he was able to test or demonstrate that the blood and brains were from the crime scene is unclear, but he declared that the blood was "not menstrual," and that both the white and blue shirtwaists and the skirt had "pure human blood and brains on them."

Perhaps the results from Metz's examination of her clothing and the knowledge that she was going to be prosecuted for murder based on them loosened her tongue. Or maybe it was the continued interrogation by LaCoste and his deputies, their use of the "third degree," and worse, the sweat box. Or the knowledge that the "Human 5" continued to kill and that telling her story would add to her legacy. Whatever her motivation, Clementine finally confessed, calling the murders her "midnight assassinations." What she confessed shocked the black quarters of the towns she had been terrorizing. Clementine Barnabet was the priestess of a murder cult, the leader of the Human Five.

Newspaper photograph of Clementine Barnabet.

I t started with a visit to a voodoo doctor in New Iberia, a town forty-five miles away from the Barnabet farm. In 1909, just before the murder of the Opelousas family in Rayne, Clementine and two men and two women traveled to acquire talismans that would protect them from detection and harm. In the newspaper accounts, those talismans were referred to as "hoodoos," "candjas," "conjah bags," "conjures," "conjuring outfit," and "voodoo charms." Clementine's was "composed of two crossed needles bound with thread and wrapped with red flannel and a few old rags."

The five of them paid $3 each for two of the voodoo doctor's talismans. They were told that the charm "would absolutely protect them from all harm and guard them from discovery in the commission of any crime or deed." But they needed to test that protection. Pushed during her confession, Clementine claimed the voodoo doctor had instructed them to commit the murders.

At first, Clementine would not identify her four accomplices, saying that the Human Five had sworn fidelity to each other. She would periodically put her head in her hands and say, "Oh, I want to tell you something but I can't."

After leaving New Iberia with the charms, the group of five drew lots to determine who would commit the first murder to test the power of their new tools. Clementine drew the first lot. She disguised herself as a man and broke into Edna Opelousas' shack in Rayne and murdered the woman and her three young children with an ax. The man that Edna's father and sister saw running south was Clementine with a man's hat in her hand. Because of her height, it would have been easy to mistake her for a man. When no one was arrested or even suspected of the grisly murder, Clementine and her conspirators decided the hoodoos had worked. Thus began the reign of terror.

Clementine carried the "talisman that rendered her impervious to harm" at all times. She even attended the funerals of some of the families she killed. When asked why the group killed children, she said, "We thought it was better to kill them all than to leave orphans, as they would suffer." This last point she contended was a tenet of her faith—that all those selected for executions must be killed, including the children so that they wouldn't suffer "from many privations."

But the identification of Clementine as the leader of the sacrificial cult and the additional arrests would not prevent the series of ax murders of more families in eastern Texas.

I magine if, in less than two years, eleven families in your general community, within a day's travel of your house, some in your own town, had been slaughtered by an ax murderer. Imagine it and you begin to understand the terror the black communities across Louisiana and eastern Texas were living with. The train tracks snaking by their homes would have been a constant reminder that the next train might deliver a killer to their backyard.

The Southern Pacific Railroad started small, in the mid-1800s, connecting California's coastal cities. Soon, though, it began acquiring small railroad companies that would extend its reach across the southern United States, companies like the Texas and New Orleans Railroad. The increased train traffic brought jobs and made interstate commerce and exporting from the west to the east and back simple. It also made it simple to export murder.

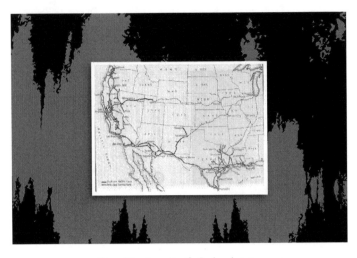

Map of Southern Pacific Railroad routes.

In her confession, Clementine told the police that there were "others who had sworn to carry out the work of extermination all along the Southern Pacific Railroad, from New Orleans to San Francisco." She warned them that the killings would continue as long as the members of her "church" kept faith in their talismans. She said that there were many families "that had been selected for killing and that their doom was sealed." The police were powerless to stop them.

Then the Monroe family was killed in Glidden, Texas, in March. Ellen Monroe was the mother of fourteen children, four of whom were with her that night. She had taken in Lyle Finucane as a boarder to help with expenses. He worked for the railroad and also had the misfortune of being home that night—he might have been followed home from work. In this case, the murderer used the ax from the family's woodpile. After entering through the back door, the killer or killers bludgeoned the family, then washed their hands on the back porch before leaving.

In April, William Burton, his wife and two children, and

his brother-in-law, Leon, were slaughtered in their sleep in San Antonio, Texas. Though axed to death, butcher knives were found sticking in all the bodies except those of the children. Another black family of "good reputation" dead at the hands of the Human Five. And just a day later, a family of three was killed in Hempstead, Texas.

There were other casualties too; people killed by accident. Shortly after the murder of the Burton family, a boy was mistaken for the killer and shot by a man guarding his house. A neighbor heard the shot and ran to investigate, but then "lost his nerve" and went back home. Other neighbors saw him, thought he was the "ax-man," and shot him as well. Both died there on the ground. In another neighborhood, a mounted policeman killed a man trying to evade arrest. His pockets were full of "voodoo lore and charms" he claimed would ward off the ax murderers.

Over forty people had been axed to death in Texas and Louisiana in the past two years. The police, the newspapers, and the community wanted to know why.

Clementine admitted to killing seventeen of the forty with her own hands. Not even out of her teens, she'd bludgeoned, hacked, and mutilated whole families, including babies, spurred by bloody, cultish beliefs.

She began to piece details together for the police. Her confession shed light on the close ties in these communities she'd been preying on. She used those ties to obscure her involvement. Of the Andrus family, she said, "I was one of the first to aid the relatives the next day and helped prepare the bodies for burial."

Clementine had also worked as a maid for a Mrs. Guidry in Lafayette. Mrs. Guidry lived one block from the Randall family. The night of that killing, Clementine used an "arc lamp" to light up the room and see the family. She stuffed rags into the keyholes, so the light wouldn't be seen. Why didn't the Randalls wake up at the light and stop her or raise the alarm?

She revealed the name of the voodoo doctor from whom they had acquired the talismans. Joseph Thibodeaux was arrested in New Iberia. When he was brought to the jail, she readily identified him, yelling, "Yes, you said that I wouldn't be arrested. But you see here I am in jail." Thibodeaux denied that he'd directed the five to murder and called Clementine "hazy and unbelievable."

He asked to be called "yarb doctah" and "mystery worker" and said that the "good white folks" of New Iberia "know him to be harmless and devoid of criminal intentions." He denied "dealing in magical charms, declaring that he was a farmer and fortune teller, using cards and reading palms." But the "mystery worker" asserted that he effected complete cures of illness by the use of roots and herbs and readily explained one of his strange plans to restore health, apparently of his own invention.

In Thibodeaux's "Cure With Paper," he would write twenty-five letters and numbers in five lines:

S.R.F. 4 A.

T.C.C.T.S.

F.W.W.U.C.

4 S.R.R.F.

A.V.O.C.S.

Thibodeaux would instruct the patient to tear off one letter, roll it into a pill, and swallow it, every time the patient felt bad. The patient would then "be cured at once of disease, domestic troubles or anything else." He also claimed that someone with this paper of letters "would never fall into the hands of his or her enemies."

Sheriff LaCoste wanted to observe secretly the "hoodoo work" of the doctor and use it as evidence to charge Thibodeaux as an accomplice to the sect murders. But he found it impossible to convince anyone to act as subjects for the doctor. Most were "too superstitious to take a chance on the effects of one of the 'conjah' man's 'spells.'"

Having nothing to hold them on, LaCoste had to release Thibodeaux and the preachers of the Church of Sacrifice. After their release, the preachers left the community. Clementine claimed that she was leader of her own cult, one predicated on human sacrifice. Its creed was the belief that only by sacrificing lives may a person gain immortality. That a young black woman of nineteen could lead a cult might have been strange in white eyes, but among practitioners of New Orleans Voodoo, priestesses were common and the legends of voodoo queens, like Marie Laveau, embodied real power.

If Clementine was the leader, she must have had followers. The police leaned on her. Who were her accomplices? Under the third degree and possibly in the sweat box, she told them about three men, two young and one old, originally living in this parish, now in Texas, but refused to give their names. At some point, she gave up a woman called "Druce," who was indignant and denied all knowledge and involvement in the murders. Clementine's brother Zepherin was pushed into a confession, and Clementine implicated another woman named Mary Cochon. The police also arrested Valena Mabry, a woman Clementine called Irene, who denied involvement.

She named several others, but none were tried and convicted for any of the murders, including her brother. Contradictory and confusing, parts of her confessions were regarded as unreliable or as an attempt to befuddle the police. As the voodoo doctor said, "hazy and unbelievable." Was the voodoo priestess working a different kind of juju on the authorities: lies and misdirection?

But if Clementine's confession is to be credited, then there were a group of people out there killing at will, united by their belief that they were protected by voodoo talismans.

Killing, perhaps, with the conviction that every bloody sacrifice made them more powerful, immortal even.

Focusing on the suspect he had in custody, though, Sheriff LaCoste believed he had enough evidence to go to trial. Clementine Barnabet, cult leader or stone-cold serial killer, was heading to the courtroom.

Judge William Campbell was no stranger to the uncanny teenage killer sitting before him in his courtroom. He had presided over the trial of her father. He'd listened to Raymond Barnabet's daughter give testimony that led to her father's conviction and could have led to the gallows.

Clementine was guarded by three deputies in the courtroom. District Attorney Howard E. Bruner decided to try her on each indictment, instead of consolidating the cases. If he didn't get a conviction on the first one, the murder of Mimi Randall, he had at least sixteen other chances. Clementine's case was one of the first tried in that fall term of the court.

The prosecution worked to link her closely with the "sacrifice sect," claiming that the group had killed three hundred people in the last six years. Whether a leader of the cult or a follower, Clementine had done her defense no favors with all the confessing she did, both to police and the press. The law gave whites legal authority over blacks when no police officer was present. When a white man showed up, even if he was just from a newspaper, in Clementine's eyes he would have been as powerful as a sheriff.

R.H. Broussard, a reporter for the *New Orleans Item*, testified that Clementine had confessed to killing the family in Rayne. That she'd done it "because a voodoo doctor had told her the officers could not get her." Broussard included a grisly detail: Clementine told him that after the murders she would "hug the dead bodies of babies to her breast."

Sheriff LaCoste, two deputies, and a doctor also testified to her confessions. Witness after witness swore that Clementine had told them the horrific details of the murders and called herself the leader. Then Bruner called Raymond Barnabet. He told the court that his daughter wasn't home the night of the Andrus murders and that it was he who had found blood on her clothing. He was demonstrably bitter, working with the prosecution, saying that Clementine "always caused him trouble."

When it was her turn to speak, Clementine yelled at the jury: "I am the axe woman of the sacrifice sect. I killed them all, men, women, and babies, and I hugged the dead babies to my breast. But I am not guilty of murder."

With Clementine actually shouting her confession into the courtroom, the defense took the only tack they had—a plea of insanity. She'd confessed to seventeen murders and the testimony in her trial showed she'd slain twenty-two. Bruner had not even called all his witnesses when he decided that he had presented enough and rested his case.

The court appointed a lunacy commission in answer to the plea of insanity. The commission was composed of two local physicians, Drs. R.D. Voorhies and John Tolson, as well as Dr. E.M. Hummel who practiced medicine in New Orleans. Hummel also sought the help of an alienist to evaluate her. From French (and originally, Latin), the term "alienist" grew out of the characterization of the mentally ill as alienated from their healthy minds. It referred both to what we would now call psychiatrists and psychologists, and it became particularly associated with those investigating the criminal mind in the legal domain. Today's forensic psychiatrists and psychologists are the descendants of the alienists of the nineteenth and early twentieth centuries. The alienist who examined Clementine Barnabet was likely often called upon to aid in the resolution of criminal cases.

In short order, the lunacy commission returned a report finding her sane. They decided that Clementine was "morally depraved, unusually ignorant and of a low grade of mentality, but not deficient in such a manner as to constitute her imbecile or idiotic." Further, they found no evidence of what they called "acquired insanity." When confronted with the possibility of a death sentence, Clementine shrugged her shoulders and said, "They can only kill me once." She told one of the physicians, "I shall have at least this satisfaction when I go, that I sent a number ahead of me."

With that information, the jury was sequestered to deliberate. While they considered her case, she sang "Nearer My God to Thee" and "Lead Kindly Light." Newspapermen gathered around her, asking questions while she puffed on a cigar one of them had given her and talked freely about the murders and her motives. Outside, members of the black community waited to hear the decision. They threatened to form a lynching party should she be acquitted. One way or another, the community wanted Clementine Barnabet to hang.

They didn't have to wait long. The jury rendered their verdict the following morning at 9 a.m. Clementine Barnabet was found guilty of killing Mimi Randall with an ax. She sat dispassionately as they read the decision, her face expressionless, her body still.

To many it seemed certain the noose was next. But instead of a death sentence, Judge Campbell sentenced her to life in prison at the Louisiana State Penitentiary at Angola, one of the most infamous jails in America, then and now.

Epilogue

Clementine said that she had expected a more severe punishment. She may not have fully understood, though, what a life sentence in Angola meant. There was one form of slavery that the Thirteenth Amendment had not made illegal: the slavery imposed as punishment for a crime.

Angola is the oldest prison farm and was at one time the largest maximum security prison in the country. Before it was converted into a prison, it was a plantation named for a region in Africa from which slaves were brought. Angola is isolated. The treacherous swamps of the Mississippi River border three sides of the prison ground. When Clementine was sent there, it was eight thousand acres. In 1922, the prison acquired ten thousand additional acres. It was later nicknamed the Alcatraz of the South. The conditions there were notoriously brutal.

Clementine began her sentence on October 29, 1912. The question of her full involvement in the murders will always remain, but shortly after she stepped into Angola, the ax murders stopped.

Clementine Barnabet represented one of the least powerful groups in Louisiana in the first decade of the twentieth century. She was a black woman. She didn't have the power to vote or hold public office. Her employment options were limited. Less than fifty years before, she would have been a slave. If she had been married off by her father, she would have effectively gone from being the property of one man to the property of another.

New Orleans Voodoo had a tremendous psychological hold on the region at the time, promising power and control. Perhaps Clementine aspired to be like the voodoo queens and priestesses that occupied the imagination of the nineteenth century American South. Maybe she saw herself as the heir to the power and legacy of women like Betsey Toledano, Sanite Dede, and the infamous Marie Laveau.

What she was able to do, if her confessions are to be believed, was terrify two states with the diabolical and merciless threat of ax murder, of being surprised while sleeping and hacked to death in bed. She rendered a white police force impotent in the face of repeated murders—at a minimum forty, but as many as three hundred over a two-year period in the southern bayou.

She fixated the public's attention squarely on the power of voodoo. There would be a correlation between the reduction of black power and the number of reports of voodoo worship. As blacks were purged from voter registration rolls and stripped of power in Louisiana, reports of voodoo rituals disappeared from white newspapers. For those two years, Clementine Barnabet kept voodoo and its threat front and center. She was powerful.

There's very little in the record about her time at Angola. The information that is available is curious. There are reports that she attempted escape a year after she was incarcerated. With alligators and copperhead snakes in the swamplands around the penitentiary, and escapees routinely drowning in the Mississippi before they could get to freedom, she must have been desperate to try to break out of Angola. Her escape attempt was unsuccessful. The punishment she received was probably vicious, given Angola's reputation for inhumane treatment.

Other sources claim she later underwent a "procedure" that turned her into a model prisoner. There are no records remaining of what the procedure was or what it entailed. The lobotomy and electroconvulsive therapy would not be commonly used in the United States until the 1930s. And though Louisiana was not one of the states that passed a law legalizing sterilization of "undesirable" populations, it's possible that such procedures were performed in the shadows of such institutions as Angola. But Clementine's transformation into a compliant prisoner might well have been due more to the draconian conditions and brutality of the Louisiana State Penitentiary than to an effective medical treatment. Those details are all that we have of Clementine's life after her conviction for ax murder.

But ten years after she entered Angola, for reasons and in conditions we don't know, Clementine Barnabet walked out of the prison. What she did and where she went is a mystery.

A Word From C.J. March

Thank you for reading *Sacrificial Axe*. If you have thoughts on this book or suggestions for other true crime accounts, please let us know at cjmarch@deadtruecrime.com. We love hearing from readers. You're why we write.

Sign up for our mailing list to learn about new Dead True Crime books and to read and listen to a free, exclusive story: www.deadtruecrime.com/ebook.

If you're interested in reading more Clementine Barnabet, check out the bibliography at the end of the book.

 facebook.com/deadtruecrime

 twitter.com/deadtruecrime

Other Dead True Crime Books

Ghoul of Grays Harbor: Murder and Mayhem in the Pacific Northwest

Sailors trusted him with their money and their lives. That was a mistake. The lucky ones woke up with headaches in the holds of ships headed to China. The others never took another breath.

Billy Gohl robbed, 'shanghaied,' and killed sailors across the Pacific Northwest. Grays Harbor in Aberdeen, Washington was so full of bodies that newspapers dubbed it a 'floaters fleet.' His trapdoor of death was famous. In his time, Gohl murdered over 100 people, making him one of the most prolific serial killers in American history.

Get Ghoul of Grays Harbor

Poison Widow
Arsenic Murders in the Jazz Age

First, she predicts your death. Then, you die. Usually, writhing in pain. Is she a fortune teller, or something much, much darker? Nobody tells the police, not for a long time, because, well, nobody in Chicago's Little Warsaw wants to cross Tillie Klimek. The body count racks up as Jazz Age Chicago's most notorious female poisoner takes down husband after husband, and some other relatives while she's at it. Few, it seems, can resist Tillie's cooking. But is this Mrs. Bluebeard working alone? Or is she part of a bigger, more diabolical "poison trust"? And can Chicago's Finest get to her before her latest husband, already mortally ill, dies? *Poison Widow* is a true-crime aficionado's feast, arsenic-laced and stuffed with tasty noir morsels.

Get Poison Widow

Murderer's Gulch
Carnage in the Catskills

Don't turn your back on her. Don't even blink. She may be crazy, but Lizzie Halliday is strong, she moves fast, and she's a stone cold killer. When famed journalist Nellie Bly interviews the woman the New York Times called "The Worst Woman on Earth," she has no idea how easy it would be for Lizzie Halliday to make Bly her next victim. In the peaceful Catskills in upstate New York, Halliday dispatches husbands, neighbors and peddlers by fire, poisoning and gunshot. The bloody death count at the Halliday farm earns it the name, "Murderer's Gulch." But even after she's arrested and committed to an insane asylum, Lizzie Halliday will kill again.

Get Murderer's Gulch

Killer Genius

The Bizarre Case of the Homicidal Scholar

He's a doctor whose patients have a way of dying; a lawyer, who uses his skills to squirm out of criminal convictions. He's a scholar, but other scholars have no idea what he's talking about. He's a family man, but one day, his wife and baby disappear forever. Only two things are clear: Edward Rulloff is a mystery, and everywhere he goes, death and destruction follow. While the criminal justice system has its hands full trying to keep and convict Edward Rulloff, the world will argue whether he's a genius, a scam artist or a madman. Even Mark Twain has an opinion.

Get Killer Genius

Coming Soon

Exit Row
Mass Murder in the Canadian Sky

A clear day. An experienced pilot. A routine flight. An obsessive love-triangle. What could go wrong? When a mysterious package follows J. Albert Guay's wife on board Flight 108, calamity is just a few ticks of the clock away. How far will a man go for his adulterous passion?

Cannibal Cowboy
Murder and Man-Eating on the American Frontier

Gold Rush and gunfights, scalping and saloons, the Old West had a reputation to uphold. But even the rough and tumble frontier wasn't ready for the likes of the Kentucky Cannibal. Mountain man and gunfighter Boone Helm would do anything to survive, right down to eating his enemies. Or his friends.

Blood Trade
Slaughter on the Underground Railroad

Nothing could be worse than slavery. Unless it was Patty Cannon hunting you down. A gang of thugs at her command, the woman infamous for her blood-thirst and brutality murdered free blacks and fugitive slaves alike for decades. Working her illegal slave trade in what became known as the Reverse Underground Railroad, Cannon's grisly tactics still have the power to chill centuries later.

About the Author

C.J. March is the alter ego of three true crime enthusiasts who wanted to write the kind of juicy noir histories they like to read. Between them they have: 2 MFAs, 3 arrests, 4 folk albums, 73 years of therapy, 1 stint working for "the artist formerly known as" which ended in a shoving match, 40 years of writing, 30 years of design, 3 dogs, and 1 overnight in a cell with a murderer.

Bibliography

"Accused Negress Laughs at Charge." *Lansing (MI) State Journal*, November 28, 1911.

"Again the Ax in Family Murders: Another Human Sacrifice Cult at Work." *Evening Herald* (Ottawa, KS), April 12, 1912.

Alexander, Michelle. *The New Jim Crow: Mass Incarceration in the Age of Colorblindness*. New York: The New Press, 2012.

"Alleged Ax Murderess Is Declared to Be Sane." *Times-Democrat* (New Orleans, LA), October 23, 1912.

"Another Butchery." *Lafayette (LA) Advertiser*, January 23, 1912.

"Arrested as Suspect." *Lafayette (LA) Advertiser*, January 23, 1912.

"Ax Fiend Again." *Lafayette (LA) Advertiser*, April 16, 1912.

"Ax Fiend at Beaumont." *Lafayette (LA) Advertiser*, February 23, 1912.

"Ax Murder's Tried Early in Fall." *Monroe (LA) News-Star*, August 20, 1912.

"Ax Murderess Sentenced." *Weekly Town Talk* (Alexandria, LA), November 2, 1912.

"'Axe-Woman' Convicted." *Times Dispatch* (Richmond, VA), October 26, 1912.

"Barnabets Probably Will Be Tried for Ax Murders." *Times-Democrat* (New Orleans, LA), October 7, 1912.

"Belief That Several Are Implicated in Murder of Family." *Town Talk* (Alexandria, LA), March 1, 1911.

"Believes Daughter." *Town Talk* (Alexandria, LA), April 10, 1912.

"Bernabet Brought Back." *Lafayette (LA) Advertiser*, September 15, 1911.

"Bernabet Convicted." *Lafayette (LA) Advertiser*, October 24, 1911.

"Bernabet Girl Guilty." *Weekly Times-Democrat* (New Orleans, LA), November 1, 1912.

"Bernabet Girl on Trial." *Times-Democrat* (New Orleans, LA), October 25, 1912.

"Bernabet Was Found Guilty." *Shreveport (LA) Times*, October 20, 1911.

"Brutal Murder." *Times-Democrat* (New Orleans, LA), November 28, 1911.

"Brutal Murder of Negro Family Is Discovered in West Crowley." *Daily Signal* (Crowley, LA), January 26, 1911.

"By Clementine Barnabet, of the 'Sacrifice Sect.'" *Fort Wayne Daily News* (IN), October 25, 1912.

"Chemist Metz Says." *Lafayette (LA) Advertiser*, January 19, 1912.

"Clementine Bernabet Sane Declared by Lunacy Commission." *Weekly Town Talk* (Alexandria, LA), October 26, 1912.

"Colored People to Aid Officers." *Crowley (LA) Signal*, January 27, 1912.

Diamond, Stephen A., PhD. "Who Were the Alienists?" *Psychology Today* (online), January 26, 2018, https://www.psychologytoday.com/ca/blog/evil-deeds/201801/who-were-the-alienists

"Doubt That One Person Could Have Butchered Six Victims." *Weekly Town Talk* (Alexandria, LA), December 9, 1911.

Elliott, Todd C. *Axes of Evil*. Waterville, OR: Trine Day, 2015.

"Fanatics Kill 35." *Washington Post*, April 13, 1912.

"Five Negroes Are Murdered in a Lake Charles Cottage." *Shreveport (LA) Times*, January 22, 1912.

"Four Beaumont Negroes Victims of the Ax Fiend Monday Night." *Crowley (LA) Signal*, February 24, 1912.

Gauthreaux, Alan G. and D.G. Hippensteel. *Dark Bayou: Infamous Louisiana Homicides.* Jefferson, NC: McFarland, 2015.

"Girl Accused Sextuple Murder." *Jackson Daily News* (MS), November 28, 1911.

Gordon, Michelle Y. "'Midnight Scenes and Orgies': Public Narratives of Voodoo in New Orleans and Nineteenth-Century Discourses of White Supremacy." *American Quarterly* 64, no. 4 (December 2012).

"Horrible Crime." *Lafayette (LA) Advertiser*, February 28, 1911.

"How the Cruel and Gruesome Murders of Africa's Wicked Serpent Worship Have Been Revived in Louisiana by a Fanatic 'Sect of Sacrifice'." *El Paso (TX) Herald*, March 14, 1912.

"Important Developments in Wholesale Butchery of Negro Family." *Weekly Town Talk* (Alexandria, LA), January 27, 1912.

"In State of Terror." *Weekly Town Talk* (Alexandria, LA), Feb 17, 1912.

"Lafayette Negroes Fear Recurrence of Mysterious Murders." *Weekly Town Talk* (Alexandria, LA), February 17, 1912.

"Life Term Given Bernabet Woman." *Times-Democrat* (New Orleans, LA), October 27, 1912.

Miller, Wilbur R., ed. *The Social History of Crime and Punishment in America.* Thousand Oaks, CA: SAGE, 2012.

"More Human Sacrifices." *Los Angeles Times,* April 13, 1912.

"Mulatto Murderess Smokes and Sings While in Jail." *Shreveport* (LA) *Times*, April 5, 1912.

"Murder in Lafayette." *Daily Signal* (Crowley, LA), February 25, 1911.

"Murder Suspect Is Jailed Here." *Crowley* (LA) *Signal*, September 9, 1911.

"Murder 'Will Out.'" *Rice Belt Journal* (Welsh, LA). January 26, 1912.

"Negress Confesses." *Lafayette* (LA) *Advertiser*, April 5, 1912.

"Negress Still Has Key to Ax Murders." *Jennings Daily* (LA) *Times-Record*, April 11, 1912.

"Negro Arrested." *Lafayette* (LA) *Advertiser*, March 28, 1911.

"Negro Family Murdered." *Lafayette* (LA) *Advertiser*, November 28, 1911.

"Negroes Fear the Ax-Men's Return." *Crowley* (LA) *Signal*, November 9, 1912.

"Negro Man, Woman and Two Children Killed with an Ax." *Times-Democrat* (New Orleans, LA), February 26, 1911.

"Negro Murderer Was Convicted." *Crowley* (LA) *Signal,* October 28, 1911.

"Negro Terror May Shorten Rice Crop." *New York Times*, March 3, 1912.

"New Ax Murder Occurs in Texas." *Times-Democrat* (New Orleans, LA), February 20, 1912.

"No Confession from Negro Girl." *Semi-Weekly Times-Democrat* (New Orleans, LA), December 1911.

"One Suspect Is Under Arrest." *Daily Signal* (Crowley, LA), January 27, 1911.

Skolnick, Jerome H. "American Interrogation: From

Torture to Trickery." In *Torture, A Collection*, edited by Sanford Levinson, Oxford: Oxford University Press, 2004.

Pendleton, Louis. "Notes on Negro Folk-Lore and Witchcraft in the South." *Journal of American Folklore* 3, no. 10 (July–September 1890).

"Quadruple Murder." *Times-Democrat* (New Orleans, LA), November 14, 1909.

"Rayne Scene of Brutal Murder." *Daily Signal* (Crowley, LA), November 13, 1909.

"Sacrifice Sect Slaughter 26." *Weekly News-Star* (Monroe, LA), January 25, 1912.

"Seek Genesis of Ax Murder Cult." *Weekly Town Talk* (Alexandria, LA), April 13, 1912.

"Shields Voodoo Slayers." *Washington Post*, April 4, 1912.

"Six Murdered in Lafayette." *Daily Signal* (Crowley, LA), November 27, 1911.

"Speedy Trial for Barnabet Woman." *Town Talk* (Alexandria, LA), April 6, 1912.

Sylvester, Richard. "A History of the 'Sweat Box' and the 'Third Degree.'" In *The Blue and the Brass: American Policing 1890-1910,* Gaithersburg, MD: IACP Press, 1976.

"Tells of Her Crimes." *Town Talk* (Alexandria, LA), October 23, 1912.

"Tells of Many Negro Murders." *Los Angeles Times*, April 3, 1912.

"The Ax Murderers Solved." *Pointe Coupee Banner* (New Roads, Louisiana), April 6, 1912.

"The Barnabet Case." *Town Talk* (Alexandria, LA), April 6, 1912.

"The Bernabet Case." *Lafayette (LA) Advertiser*, April 9, 1912.

"Voodoo Doctor Caught." *Town Talk* (Alexandria, LA), April 4, 1912.

"Warner Murder Still a Mystery." *Daily Signal* (Crowley, LA), January 20, 1912.

Wayside Notes Along the Sunset Route, Westbound. San Francisco: Southern Pacific, 1911.

"Wholesale Murders Cause Panic Among the Colored Inhabitants." *Daily Signal* (Crowley, LA), January 22, 1912.

Wilson, Charles Reagan, and Amy Louise Wood, eds. *The New Encyclopedia of Southern Culture: Volume 19. Violence.* Chapel Hill, NC: University of North Carolina Press, 2011.

"Woman Confesses to Killing 17 Negroes." *New York Times*, April 3, 1912.

"Zepherin Barnabet Says He Took Part in Murders." *Weekly Times-Democrat* (New Orleans, LA), April 26, 1912.

Image Credits

CHAPTER 3

Newspaper photograph of the Andrus home. Courtesy *Utica Saturday Globe*, February 1912.

Photograph of Sheriff Louis LaCoste. Courtesy LafayetteSheriff.Com, Lafayette Parish Sheriff's Office.

CHAPTER 5

Newspaper photograph of the Randall home. Courtesy *Utica Saturday Globe*, February 1912.

CHAPTER 6

Newspaper illustration of voodoo rituals. Courtesy *El Paso Herald*, March 14, 1912.

CHAPTER 7

Newspaper drawing of Broussard victim's hand. Courtesy *El Paso Herald*, March 14, 1912.

CHAPTER 9

Newspaper photograph of Clementine Barnabet. Courtesy *The Constitution* (Atlanta, GA), April 7, 1912.

CHAPTER 10

Map of Southern Pacific Railroad routes. Courtesy PSRM.Org, Pacific Southwest Railway Museum.

Slingshot Books

Minneapolis

www.slingshotbooks.com

57079803R00046

Made in the USA
Middletown, DE
26 July 2019